WITHDRAWN
FROM
STOCK

a girl's guide to
etiquette

a girl's guide to
etiquette

sandra deeble

illustrations by *chris long*

RYLAND
PETERS
& SMALL

LONDON NEW YORK

Designer Sarah Fraser
Commissioning Editor Annabel Morgan
Production Paul Harding
Art Director Gabriella Le Grazie
Publishing Director Alison Starling

*First published in the United Kingdom
in 2004 by Ryland Peters & Small
Kirkman House
12–14 Whitfield Street
London W1T 2RP
www.rylandpeters.com*

*Text, design and illustrations
© Ryland Peters & Small 2004*

10 9 8 7 6 5 4 3 2 1

Printed and bound in China

ISBN 1 84172 736 9

contents

introduction

Etiquette is hip. Etiquette is sexy. Etiquette is knowing what to do when and how to do it... and I'm not talking white gloves, lace handkerchiefs or being canny with cutlery. Etiquette *de nos jours* is about appropriate responses to modern dilemmas, while always considering other people's feelings along the way. Girls who are at one with modern etiquette are successful, confident, popular and at one with themselves. Frankly, etiquette is essential.

However, traditional etiquette often doesn't quite hit the mark with the way we live today. And what a relief that all those old rules can be ignored. Having said that, we seem to spend far more time and energy now figuring out how to behave in unknown situations or ever-shifting work and social landscapes. As a result, we waste valuable energy thinking 'Should I call so-and-so and explain that I didn't really mean it like that?'.

While most of us are confident that we can enjoy shiraz with seared salmon and not give two hoots for archaic by-the-book-dom, it's pretty clear that an up-to-date guide to etiquette for today's gorgeous girl is needed.

These days a thoroughly modern Ms needs to be as well versed in subjects as diverse as netiquette and when to go Dutch, to how to organize a hen weekend or compose a letter to a friend whose parent has just died. This guide will stand you in good stead. You'll win  friends and wow the world. Do what comes naturally, but do it with grace, charm, good manners and a sincere smile. A smile that comes from a well-mannered, kind and considerate heart.

Enjoy etiquette. It's fun, it makes life easier – you'll be able to waltz through life. You'll make up-hill struggles look like sexy slaloms and everyone will secretly wonder which charm school you went to. Party invitations will crowd your letterbox, perfect jobs will land in your lap and you'll never need botox to iron out those furrows in your brow. (Wondering about how best to handle a tricky situation is known to be the greatest cause of wrinkles, don't you know!) So enjoy this guide. Adapt the advice to suit you, by all means, then go forth and shimmy and sparkle your way through life.

everyday *etiquette*

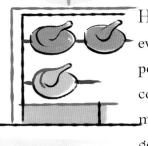

How do you like to be treated? Have you ever felt annoyed or upset by other people's thoughtlessness and lack of consideration? Are you a model of good manners? Most of the time? Or only on good hair days? Charming, popular girls know it's best to treat people in the way they like to be treated themselves. And when faced with rudeness or bad manners, it's easier and less stressful to smile sweetly and rise above it all.

communication

I love the fact that when we all first became addicted to email, the Royal Mail reported a dramatic increase in the number of handwritten letters. Now, I'm not saying that we should all reject Outlook Express and opt for Smythson (or Basildon Bond) – far from it.

But what I do think is fantastic is that our approach to communication is so eclectic and constantly evolving. Yes, our grandparents might still sit down with their writing paper and fountain pen, but they're also texting their grandchildren. I suppose the most refreshing recent development is that people have admitted that just because they can communicate with anyone, anywhere, at anytime, it doesn't mean that it's always desirable or appropriate. 'No internal email days' are now being trialled in offices. And the 'I can even take my laptop to the beach!' school of thought has been tempered by the realization that sometimes it is actually good to switch off for a while...

So here follows a few thoughts on the etiquette of contemporary communications:

It's good to talk, but...

It's surprising how many people seem to think it's acceptable to spend the evening out with a group of people, yet spend most of the night chatting animatedly on a mobile phone. This is not acceptable behaviour! If you find yourself spending more time talking on your mobile than to the person you're with, maybe you should arrange to meet again when you can pay them more attention. On the subject of mobiles, don't expect people to call you for long chats on your mobile. Offer to call them back or give them a land line number if you're near a phone. If you're talking to someone on your home or office phone and your mobile rings, leave it. Do not try to have two conversations at once. It's rude!

'I sent you an email but it bounced back'

Don't forward personal emails to other friends. They'll start wondering whether their emails to you are sent on to other people. Do let people know if your computer's 'coming down with something'. And always think before you click send!

'It's exactly what I wanted!'

When it comes to presents, I think that thank you letters are a good thing. If this seems too formal for your social scene, a thank-you email or text will suffice. It's perfectly acceptable for parents to write on their children's behalf until the kids can put pencil to paper themselves. That 'I love my *Babar* book' from a one year old isn't necessary. Before children become fully fledged wordsmiths, drawings are lovely.

Mwah! Mwah!

If in doubt, always offer your hand first, rather than going for a kiss with a complete stranger. Having said that, quite often you'll meet someone new, shake hands, then once you become intimate (after a two-minute conversation) you'll air-kiss them goodbye. When it comes to single, double or even triple kissing, the jury is out. It depends on age, how the person is feeling and where they come from. As a rule of cheek, take it slowly. It's when the speed picks up and you go for three kisses but the other person stops after two that you both end up with banged noses. And I don't know whether it's a right-handed thing or not, but most people do tend to proffer their right cheek first.

'This old thing?'

If you can't take a compliment graciously, start practising now. If you don't believe someone and think they're being insincere, that's your problem. 'Thank you', and nothing else, is the correct response to a compliment. Not 'Do you need your eyes tested?' or 'You're only saying that'. And make sure you tell people all the good things you think about them, rather than just thinking them!

out and about

Awareness is key when you're out and about. Self-awareness is one thing, but you've already got a mini library of self-help manuals for that. I'm talking about being aware of other people. If we all wandered around totally caught up in our own thoughts or making mental 'to do' lists, the number of accidents would soar!

Public transport

Be aware of anyone who might appreciate being offered your seat. I'm amazed at how many heavily pregnant women and elderly people are left standing just because nobody has noticed them.

Behind the wheel

However inconsiderate another driver might be, do not under any circumstances use your horn! Remember, you are far too sleek, superior and well-mannered. Always give way to horses, buggies, prams, pedestrians and cyclists. Do not, under any circumstances, get impatient and threaten to mow them down in your 4 x 4.

Trains

People do all sorts of strange things on trains. More room to roam around in means people often adopt a 'make yourself at home' approach, particularly on long journeys. That's fine... but do keep your feet off the seats, don't eat disgusting burgers (or any other smelly food) and please don't have loud arguments on your mobile.

On foot

Don't push in front of people – at a zebra crossing, or entering a shop – and step aside if someone looks intent on a head-on collision. Be careful with umbrellas, backpacks or hefty handbags. They can be lethal.

Shopping

If there's an ownerless trolley standing by the checkout, it's probably because its owner has suddenly remembered they wanted coriander and rushed back to the fruit and veg section. Be kind! What about the time you realized you needed filo pastry just as the cashier was about to swipe your card and everyone was tut-tutting? Other rules: do not attempt to sneak a trolley into the 'basket only' queue. You're asking for trouble. And when it comes to the deli counter, think of queuing as a form of Zen meditation. Wear a beatific smile and queue serenely.

Cinemas, theatres, opera houses...

Don't forget you're in a public place and you're here to enjoy a shared experience. If you want to discuss what's happening on screen with your companion, go home and wait until it comes out on video. Keep your opinions to yourself during the film. Instead, discuss them afterwards in a pseudo-intellectual way while sipping red wine. Even if the film you've just seen happens to be Thunderbirds.

In-flight etiquette

Don't fall asleep on the stranger next to you, snuggle into their shoulder or dribble on their jacket. Don't file your nails or brush your hair all over someone. And if someone doesn't want to chat, leave them alone.

restaurants

Q: Sometimes I want to complain in a restaurant, but I don't want to cause an unpleasant scene.

A: Why do we associate complaining with causing a scene? It doesn't have to lead to an unpleasant altercation. Done in the right way, complaining can be very constructive – think of it as drawing someone's attention to a negative point or potential problem. Arctic air-conditioning, deafening 'background' music, dirty cutlery, corked wine, wrong orders, cold food or finding that your 'seafood something' contains one solitary prawn are all absolutely valid grounds for complaint in a restaurant. The 'Excuse me, but can you explain why/how?' approach, accompanied by a charming smile, is always a good ploy.

Many people lose all sense of right, wrong and assertiveness when they're out for the evening. Remember, you're paying! We all need to complain if necessary, to raise standards and challenge the perception that complaining is obnoxious. Constructive complaining helps people make their businesses better, and potentially more successful.

Q: I went out for a meal with a group of friends, and because I'd been ill the week before I drank only mineral water and ordered clear soup. The others all had three courses and ordered lobster and oysters. When the bill arrived, they wanted to split it equally. I paid up without arguing, but felt angry and exploited afterwards.

A: The 'splitting the bill' problem often causes resentment or bad feeling. It's a slate-grey matt surface in the vibrant, glossy world of hip etiquette. People tend to feel short-changed when they order modestly or only have one course when everyone else had three. But unfortunately, this is just one of those situations where you have to grin and bear it. Good manners dictate that you can't squabble over your share of the bill or demand to pay less, unless someone else in the party suggests it. The onus is on the person who organized the get-together to point out that you ate and drank considerably less than everyone else and therefore should pay a reduced amount. The only solution is either not to join in group outings, or to cram down three courses and guzzle a bottle of wine if you need to feel that you've got your money's worth!

Q: Is tipping archaic?

A: No! Tipping is alive and kicking. The figure 10 per cent still continues to float around, but the reality is that many restaurants nowadays automatically add a $12\frac{1}{2}$ per cent service charge to your bill, particularly if there are more than six people in your party. Other restaurants are content to simply stamp 'Service Not Included' on the bill and to leave a blank line on your credit card slip so you can fill in a tip if you want to. Some establishments add a service charge to the bill AND a blank line to credit card slips, with the result being that some people end up tipping 25 per cent or more, completely unawares. This is rude and sneaky behaviour and should be stopped!

If you are happy with the service you have received, tip at least 10 per cent or more. Unless you really want to make a point, don't start faffing by changing the $12\frac{1}{2}$ per cent service charge to 10 per cent! If you feel that the service was so poor that your server doesn't deserve a tip, deduct the service charge from the bill – but explain why, either to your waiter or the manager. If you don't, people will just think that you're tight-fisted and the service will never improve.

personal *etiquette*

It's not every day that you bump into a Marchioness or an Admiral. So don't waste time worrying about how to address them. Hitting the right notes with your friends, family and lovers can be even more difficult. When you're relaxed, it's easy to drop your Ps and Qs or to be overly frank, causing offence without intending to. And that's before you've even agreed whose turn it is to host Christmas!

friends and family

The closer you are to someone, the more likely that common courtesy is forgotten. This person knows you, warts and all, so why be on your best behaviour? Relax! Burp, fart, swear, tell them the truth! After all, they asked for your advice and added 'Be brutal'. Yes, it's good to be honest, but do spare a thought for the feelings of others. However 'yourself' you can be with someone, it's best to try walking in the other person's shoes to see how it feels.

Q: I have a sneaking suspicion that my friend's boyfriend fancies me. What do you suggest?

A: If he makes a pass at you, tell him in no uncertain terms that his advance isn't welcome. Don't tell your friend.

Q: I've got a friend who's becoming a 'frenemy'. I don't know what to do. Is it possible to 'dump' a friend?

A: Yes, it is, but it's not easy. Sometimes friendships run past their sell-by date and fizzle out naturally. But sometimes friendships limp on, with neither person wanting to 'finish' it. Advocates of clutter-clearing are all for friendship pruning, brutal as that may sound. If you really want to distance yourself from a friend, my advice is to slowly put less effort into a friendship, so gradually you drift apart.

With true friends, obviously, there are times when one of you is giving more than the other, and this is how it should be – so please don't give up on friends who genuinely need you.

Q: I recently asked a friend's friend whether she kept in touch with her ex. As I said it (and she replied 'no way!') I remembered he had had an affair with someone. What a stupid question! I realized I'd upset her. Should I call her and apologise?

A: No! It'll only make it worse! Best to leave it alone. If you see her again soon, you can apologize face-to-face. If a phone call veers off track unexpectedly, it's always best to leave the dust to settle. If you call back immediately, the danger is that the person may just be getting back to neutral with the help of a large glass of wine, when all of a sudden you make them plumb the depths again!

Q: My friend recently split up with her boyfriend and we all joined in the 'he wasn't right for you' game. They're now back together and are getting married! I wish I hadn't said some of the things I did...

A: Oh dear – it's a bit late now isn't it?! You'll know better next time. When friends split up, it's best to say nothing against the person who's been dumped or has done the dumping. Support your friend, that's all you need to do. Listen, don't judge. It's harder than it sounds!

Q: I asked a friend: 'Are you going to Matt and Kay's party at the weekend?' The stunned silence made me realize that she hadn't been invited. I felt dreadful...
A: It happens. It's not your fault. You can only apologise for upsetting your friend unintentionally.

Q: A close friend had a baby recently. I was devastated because I found out from another friend that the baby had arrived. She received a round-robin email and I wasn't on the list.
A: It was probably an oversight. Most likely your friend got her husband to do the email and he cocked up. Call her – it'll be fine.

Q: My friend has asked me to be godmother to her baby daughter. I feel awkward about all the religious stuff. What should I do?
A: Tell your friend that you're ill at ease with the 'pastoral care' part of the role, and she'll probably tell you that she wants you to be a godparent because you're fab and groovy, you'll give great gifts and will be an inspiring role model!

Q: My sister has gone ahead and bought a computer for my dad for Christmas. She now wants me to 'come in' with her and has said that because I earn more, I should pay two thirds. Is this fair?
A: No, of course it isn't, but what is ever fair with siblings? Argue the toss if you want to, but if you can easily afford it, it might be worth paying an unfair share just to avoid any frostiness at Christmas.

lovers

You've read The Rules *and ripped them up. You think that you're relatively savvy. Yet most of us still feel awkward when it comes to those bill-paying and 'D'you want to come in for coffee?' moments. Here are some of the most common questions about dating:*

Q: Is it acceptable for a girl to ask a boy out?
A: Yes. It is perfectly proper. Inviting someone to go somewhere or do something specific is always a good strategy.

Q: What is the best way for a girl to prepare for a first date?
A: By plucking, tweaking, prinking and polishing her body to within an inch of its life. Think glam... think gorgeous!

Q: Should I dress to flirt on a first date?
A: You should always dress to flirt!

Q: Who should pay on a first date?
A: If he's suggested it and chosen the venue, then it's perfectly acceptable for him to pay. Rather than looking as if you're expecting him to pay, offer to pay half, then thank him graciously when he refuses.

You can pay next time. Some people prefer to go Dutch if they know there's never going to be a second date!

Q: Supposing I need to cancel the first date?

A: Call him and explain the situation. Don't cancel by email. You'll spend all day worrying if he got the message, or whether he's out of the office all day and was planning to come straight to meet you after work.

Q: What about phoning him during the early stages?

A: Absolutely fine, no matter what anyone else tells you. But if you have the odd wobble when self confidence leaves you, you might like to let him make the next call, after which your confidence will come back in lorry-loads.

Q: Is it OK to have sex on the first date?

A: Of course it is. But if you think you might crumble the morning after and start worrying about whether you should have waited, then it's always better to wait.

Q: How long do you think I should I leave it before making the follow-up call after the first time we have sex?

A: 24 hours. If you feel shy, this is often easier done by email.

Q: What do I do when I finally get to meet his parents and his dad makes a pass at me?

A: Snub him – hard. Even if his dad looks like a mature George Clooney. Say: 'I don't think this is appropriate, do you?'

Q: How should I end it?

A: Firstly, don't dump by text. It is rude, shabby and cowardly. Secondly, don't dump by email, for the same reasons.

Q: Face to face is better then?

A: Every time. You meet, you have the big chat and get through the tears, recriminations and the 'what about the dog?' questions. Don't be persuaded into changing your mind. And remember, whatever happens, it is not appropriate to indulge in, or agree to, closure sex.

Q: What about dividing up all our stuff?

A: If a Jiffy bag arrives in the post a few days later containing the spare set of keys you'd given him, that's all well and good. But if the Paul Smith cufflinks you bought for his birthday are also returned, this is rude, very rude. Do not return presents, it's unkind. You know better.

workplace *etiquette*

Trampling over people to get to the top is not big and it's not clever. Don't even attempt to play a dirty game. Charm and consideration for both superiors and minions are what count in the workplace and, given that genuine kindness is so rare, if you do display impeccable manners, you will shimmy your way to the top effortlessly.

jobs

It's a crowded market and you are a brand that needs to stand out as an aspirational, clearly positioned and highly polished product. Here are some of the questions that you may have spent time pondering:

Q: Are CVs still important?
A: Yes. You need one, and it goes without saying that it has to be brilliant. Clear, concise and well-designed; with perfect spelling and grammar, and tailored for each job you apply for. The same goes for covering letters. And don't expect to hear back from people. Instead, you need to follow up. Even more important is networking. That's how people get the good jobs. Know your market. Talk to people and make an effort with everyone.

Q: I've got a really important interview coming up next week and I haven't got a clue what to wear. Please can you help?
A: You could do a discreet recce by going to the venue and checking out people as they leave the building after work. Try to gauge what the dress code is at the new organization, and then up the ante for the interview. You can relax a little once you've got your feet under the table.

Q: I was drafting a jokey email to a guy I fancy, but I accidentally hit 'send' and it went to a client instead. Help!

A: Well, you could do nothing and say nothing and just sit tight and see if the client mentions it. Sometimes it makes matters worse by drawing someone's attention to an email faux pas. Otherwise, be bold, call the client straight away and say 'Sorry, I just don't know what happened there.' Spare him any long-winded explanations.

Q: Parsnip, my Jack Russell, gets lonely at home. Could I take him into the office? He's really well-behaved!

A: There is an official 'Bring your dog to work day'. Take Parsnip in on that day, by all means. Otherwise, it very much depends on how your co-workers take to doggy smells around the photocopier. A scented candle may help.

Q: The air conditioning in our office is temperamental. What about wearing shorts in summer?

A: No way! Are you a courier? Think linen shift dresses or demure knee-length skirts. And on no account should you

bare your midriff, no matter how flat and tanned it is. As for low-slung trousers with thongs a go-go, it's just not nice to show your pants to the world, so please sort yourself out.

Now then, let's move on to footwear. Teetering strappy sandals are more nightclub than workplace, and tend to give the wrong impression. Whatever your footwear, pedicures in summer are mandatory, that goes without saying. Gunky gnarled toes are so unattractive.

Q: Rosie, who I work quite closely with, asked me what I thought about Pip, another girl in the office. I felt awkward. Any advice?

A: Stay neutral, gorgeous girl! It's imperative that you do not sully yourself with nasty nattering or bitchy behaviour – it's beneath you and won't win you any friends.

Q: I've been promoted and I'm nervous. How will my co-workers take to me suddenly being their boss?

A: As a new broom, it's best not to sweep in too briskly. Gently does it. Be compassionate. Take things slowly. Put yourself in the shoes of your colleagues and act with sensitivity. But

don't forget, you are now the boss and you will have to behave like one. It may sound boring, but adopting a pleasant, firm manner will win you more respect than trying to stay everybody's best friend.

Q: I really fancy this project manager called Archie. Should I make a move?

A: Hmm. Office affairs can be messy things, especially as they have a funny habit of becoming common knowledge. And it can be hard to get over a break up when the object of your affections is sitting at the next desk all day, every day. Having said that, office affairs can also be good things, with you both ending up happy ever after. Just remember, they should only be conducted with single colleagues. Not married ones. And preferably not your boss. (Although that particular match can also have a happy ending.)

Q: Is the stationery cupboard really the best place for office sex?

A: No! Don't have sex in the stationery cupboard! It's dangerous. If things get too heated a box of jiffy bags might fall on your head and cause concussion.

elegant
entertaining

If you are a girl who knows how to enjoy herself, the likelihood is that you will instinctively know how to give other people a good time. Just think about how you would like to be invited, greeted, fed, watered and treated. Then do unto others... and before you know it, you'll find yourself on the Most Gorgeous Hostess shortlist!

invitations

If in doubt about whether to telephone, email or send proper invitations, stop to think for a moment. How do you feel when you receive an invitation in the post? Are you excited? Do you think 'how nice to be asked' and 'can't wait'? Do you immediately start to wonder about what you should wear? Written invitations always create a feeling of anticipation and excitement.

Personally, I love real party invitations to events that are truly social (as opposed to work-related, networking or book launch events). When a friend is having a big bash, or I've been invited to a wedding, a christening or a birthday party, I always feel elated and the invitation goes straight on the mantelpiece. If you do receive an invitation by post, you must always respond in writing, unless the RSVP is followed by a phone number.

These days, email invitations are increasingly popular, particularly in the form of round robins for barbecues, mulled wine and mince pie parties, and a host of other informal get-togethers. It's absolutely fine to accept email by email. As a hostess, you will have to live with it if not everyone responds. You might end up ringing round to find out if the email arrived so, all things considered, you might just as well put something in writing, post it and have done with it.

Engraved, thermographed or flat printed? If you don't know the difference, just skip this section. But when it comes to traditional wedding etiquette, there are three ways to go. Posh people detest thermography and always go for engraved invites. Mere mortals are usually just pleased to have been asked and don't waste precious energy checking to see whether the print is raised or not. And if you're organizing a wedding in your own inimitable style, then you will probably create something with an incredibly individual and stylish twist. It's essential to be clear in the wording of your invitation. If it's a grown up affair and you don't want children, say so. If you want a cut-off point, spell it out. Send a map if necessary.

Here are a few ideas for wording invitations:

At last! The builders have left and we invite you to warm up our cool, understated space.

Sunday 28 September

Midday onwards

4 Alexandra Road

Kate and Matt

*R.S.V.P. 020 8123 4567;
kateandmatt@anynet.com*

Matt invites you to help him let down what little is left of his hair to celebrate his 40th birthday.

He promises to play music you will recognize and to provide chairs that are comfortable

*Saturday 14 June
4 Alexandra Road*

8pm

*R.S.V.P. 020 8987 6543;
mattmills@internet.com*

Lola invites you to tango for no reason

*on
Saturday 24 May
7pm*

72 London Road

*Running order:
7pm drinks
8pm tango class
9pm party
and practise your new moves*

Dress: red and black

how to be a
gorgeous hostess

* Make people your tippety top priority.

* If you want to have a dress code, choose one your guests will find it fun to adhere to, rather than a chore. For example: 'Dress to flirt', 'Dress to boogie', 'Be glam'.

* Look relaxed and be happy to see your guests when they arrive. There's nothing worse than being greeted by a stressed hostess who says, 'I'm in such a state, it's all gone pear-shaped,' as she reels off a list of behind-the-scenes disasters.

* Think about who you've invited and how to get people mingling. Introduce people as soon as they arrive, giving them a handy hook to kick things off with.

* Get up early the day before the party and go to a flower market. Even if you can't get to a market, buy flowers the day before and they'll be perfect by the time of the party.

* Set the scene with lighting. Turn off or dim the ceiling lights and opt for tea lights, church candles or lanterns – candlelight is always flattering and atmospheric.

* Play music! Stony silences will make everybody cringe.

* Make the room smell gorgeous. No horrible air fresheners!
  Scented candles made with essential oils are the way to go.

* Provide yummy nibbles (and no, I'm not talking twiglets).
  Even a big wooden bowl of kettle chips or giant olives
  show that you're making an effort. A cereal bowl of dry
  roasted peanuts simply does not pass muster.

* Serve delectable drinks. It's better to keep things simple
  and have a limited list, be it pomegranate martinis,
  champagne or mugs of hot chocolate. Avoid serving too
  many strong drinks before dinner: your guests will peak too
  early and by the time they eat they'll
  be tired and emotional.

* Have lots of non-alcoholic drinks on
  offer. It's amazing how much trouble
  people go to choosing wine then
  only offer warm tap water to non-
  drinkers. As hostess, the temptation is
  to get wasted because you don't have to go anywhere.
  Drink some water every now and again.

* Think about the individual needs of your guests. Ashtrays (or a balcony and blanket) for smokers. Somewhere comfy to sit for your heavily pregnant friend who's insisted on wearing heels for cocktails but has gone as far as she can for the sake of style.

* Depending on the scale of your event, remember to warn/invite your neighbours.

* Look delighted when guests arrive bearing a classy bottle of Chablis. But also be gracious enough to act delighted when presented with a cheap bottle of plonk from the corner shop, while pressing on with the rather tasteful Tasmanian pinot noir you have chosen to go with the food you've prepared. Depending on the success of the evening, the plonk may come in handy at 2am when you're playing truth or dare and you've already drained a bottle of Metaxa you bought in Duty Free after your holiday in Skiathos 6 years ago.

* If you're having a dinner party, lay the table the night before. It sounds staid, but it works.

* Keep the food simple. Don't plan meals where you're in the kitchen desperately trying to cook four different things all at the last minute. This always leads to huge gaps between courses, while your guests get more and more plastered.

* Ask people beforehand if they're vegetarians, have any wheat or nut allergies or a recent addiction to Atkins.

* If you're doing a table plan, think it through carefully. Mix up shy and boisterous people to avoid having a lopsided lunch.

* Accept help gracefully. (But only from friends who will be a genuine help, rather than a hindrance!)

* Nurture healthy debate, but if it gets out of hand and two of your guests are about to step outside, you are the hostess and it's your duty to put a stop to it.

* Don't start clearing up while people are obviously still enjoying themselves. Loud clattering washing-up sounds from the kitchen kill the atmosphere stone dead.

* You're a gorgeous hostess, but you're knackered. 'School tomorrow!' is a failsafe way to galvanize people to make tracks. Far better to admit that you're exhausted and need to get to bed than noisily plate-stacking in the kitchen, which is the rude way of getting people to leave.

* Have a taxi number to hand. And warn people if there is likely to be a long wait. There's nothing worse than winding things up and saying your goodbyes then making polite conversation for the next hour while you wait for the taxi to actually arrive.

* The 'don't smile before Christmas' advice for new teachers can be adapted for gorgeous hostesses. Don't think about enjoying yourself before pudding, or until the dance floor is full.

the art of conversation

'So what do YOU do?' is, more often than not, the very first question we ask after we've established someone's name. I went on a yoga holiday in Greece where everyone was banned from talking about their jobs. For the first few minutes, people were literally lost for words, readjusting themselves to this new conversational etiquette. And then... the miracle happened! Genuinely interesting and original conversations took place. People said later they had talked about things that had never crossed their minds before. The downside of this, obviously, was that most of us spent the entire fortnight being Miss Marple, trying our damnedest to find out what people really did back home. Without going to those yogic extremes to make you feel karma about meeting strangers, here are a few tips to boost your social confidence:

* Always always always smile and look approachable.

* If you find yourself at a do where you know nobody, or you can't find the person who invited you, get yourself a drink, then look out for someone on their own and try to find out how they know the host, if indeed they do. They could be a gatecrasher, which might even prove more interesting!

* Listen to what the other person is saying.

* When you do get talking to someone, don't avoid the so-called 'boring' topics. The weather, holidays, something you've just heard on the news on the way there (anything from the latest celeb gossip to a fad diet or whether organic chocolate really does add va-va-voom to your sex drive) are all perfectly acceptable.

* Ask about things the other person is interested in. Question them gently... without turning into Jeremy Paxman.

* Are silences grim or golden? Rather than rushing to fill the void, try sitting out the silence. Sometimes the other person will have the confidence to say something stunning. Or not, as the case may be...

* If the person you're talking to makes you feel desperate, try the following: 'Will you excuse me, I've just seen George and he looks as if he's about to leave. I must catch him!' Or this: 'I'm going for a top up, would you like another drink?' (When you return from the bar, pretend you've met someone else en route, and that you're only delivering the drink, not about to resume the dire chat.)

* Heavenly hostesses 'rescue' people who get stuck. As a guest, you could pretend to see someone who needs rescuing and save yourself at the same time.

* Nibble the nibbles, be they Twiglets or sushi, but avoid getting so involved with the miniature morsels that your mouth is actually too full to answer a question!

how to be a good guest

'Sit down! Just enjoy yourself!' It sounds a bit rude, doesn't it? After all, you were only trying to help. Yet many a guest has been rebuffed in this way. Good guest etiquette is one of those areas where you have to take the temperature of things on arrival and adapt your philosophy to suit. Here are a few do's and don'ts that might help you on your way.

* Do respond quickly to invitations. If you can't go, don't fancy it, or feel that so much is going on in your life that you'll arrive feeling stressed and strung out, say so. Don't accept invites to things you don't want to go to, it's worse than not going at all. And be honest about why you can't go...without hurting the feelings of the hostess.

* Don't hedge your bets. There's nothing worse than making your hostess nervous by keeping your options open. Some people are notorious for this, leaving it to the last moment before accepting to see if they get any better offers. This is hideous behaviour!

* Traditional etiquette frowned upon guests arriving with a present for their hosts. You didn't see Maggie Smith turning up at Gosford Park with a couple of bottles of Chilean Red under her arm, did you? Happily, today things are different. Would you be offended if your friend arrived for dinner bearing gifts? I don't think so.

* Do offer to help beforehand. Keep it simple. Say: 'Do you want me to bring anything?' or 'Is there anything I can do to help?'.

* Do let people know if you're going to be late. (as early as possible, if that makes any sense).

* Do immediately offer to pay for anything you inadvertently break or ruin. And please keep your children under control. Some people let their little darlings run amok and then look dismayed when Ribena gets spilled on the cream velvet sofas. A particularly irksome spin on this scenario is when your own possessions get damaged during a social call. If something precious gets ruined and the guilty party offers to pay, accepting graciously is the only way to go.

* Do ask if you can help. But don't get into an awkward tussle over a damp tea towel. If your hostess says: 'No, sit down, you're a guest!' do as she says. Unless you know her very very well indeed and you know that she's being polite. But this is where faux politeness trips us all up, leaving us confused and miserable. As a rule of thumb, you have to believe what people tell you, it's generally the only way to go.

* Don't loll around like an Edwardian lady while your friend tries to make supper, bath three children and answer the phone. Offer to stir the risotto, it's the least you can do.

* Don't make a mess, phone your best mate in Melbourne, help yourself to food or crack open expensive bottles of wine they were saving for a special occasion.

* Don't outstay your welcome! As a rule, gorgeous girls always leave their hosts begging for more.

* Do say thank you and let your host or hostess know how much you appreciated their efforts. Traditional etiquette demands a thank-you letter written the next day, but nowadays, it depends on your social circle. Depending on the occasion, you should either write, send a card, text, email or call.

Good presents

* Flowers are always lovely to receive, but some people think that it's a hassly present, because the hostess has to stop hostessing in order to faff around finding vases and cutting stems. If you anticipate such shenanigans, take flowers already arranged in a simple glass vase. Or bung them in a jug or the bath yourself. No doubt she'll enjoy them after you've gone.

* Exquisite foodstuffs are always acceptable, especially something utterly drop-dead delicious. It's always easy to think of edible offerings for ex-pats, but also buy exotic goodies that friends might not have on their doorstep. Beautiful wrapping makes a big difference too, showing that you've really made an effort.

* Finally, the best guests bring new energy into the home of the host or hostess. Get involved with what's going on, don't think about all the things you've got to do in your own life and contribute some of your own spirit, in addition to whatever you happen to have brought in a bottle!

formal *occasions*

No matter how confidently we eschew etiquette, when it comes to births, deaths and marriages, the tendency is to come over all proper. Trad with a twist might be the order of the day, yet as we fight to defy convention, there are nevertheless certain rules that continue to rule. Ignore them at your peril. Or better still, know them inside out, then break them with panache!

weddings

Apart from your funeral, this is perhaps the only day in your life when you're going to get every single one of your friends, from every stage of your life, all together under one roof dancing to Abba. Yippee! Before you start to display signs of advanced control freakery and develop a hectoring tone with everyone (including your husband-to-be) here are a few important things to consider:

* Don't feel under pressure to invite people. Your friend may have just met her dream man, but will he stick around forever and do you want his mug in your wedding shots? The same goes for work colleagues. It's your wedding, not an opportunity to network.

* Spare a thought for guests. Some serial guests claim that they can no longer afford to go on holidays – they have become professional wedding tourists as more and more of their friends choose far-flung exotic destinations to get hitched. Be sensitive!

* On the work front, most brides spend lots of time organizing anything from body wraps to salsa lessons during work time. People soon tire of this. So be discreet.

* Choose your wedding team with care. Bridesmaids and readers need to be able to deliver, not dry up on the day!

Invitations

The most traditional style of invitation comes from the parents of
the bride and begins *'Mr and Mrs James Henry request the pleasure...'*.
If the parents are divorced and the mother has remarried, then it
would begin: *'Mr James Henry and Mrs Peter Valentine...'* If the mother
has not remarried then it is: *'Mr James Henry and Mrs James Henry...'*.
The guest's name is usually handwritten in the top left-hand corner.
This is where people come over all fancy with gold ink and flourishes
and calligraphy. If you have a wedding list, don't enclose it with the
invitation – it's not good etiquette. Guests can ask you whether you
have a list, and where it is. Below is the traditional wedding invitation
wording and a less standard approach:

Mr and Mrs James Henry
request the pleasure of your company
at the marriage of their daughter

Amanda Jane
to
Mr Martin Sadler

at St Mary's Church, Norwich

on Saturday 18th October 2003
at 3 o'clock

and afterwards at The Mad Moose,
Norwich

R.S.V.P.
23 Primrose Gardens
Norwich, Norfolk

If you and your husband to be are
hosting the event, then
you would begin:

'Amanda Henry and Martin Sadler
request the pleasure
of your company at their marriage
at St Mary's Church...'

How to be the best 'best woman'

It's nice to be asked, but if you feel uncomfortable about taking on this role, say so. As the day draws near you will regret it if you felt weird about the whole thing to start with. If you're game, however, go for it lock, stock and barrel.

Speeches

I find it odd that in this day and age some brides remain mute as they gaze adoringly at their new husbands. But then some brides hate speaking in public at the best of times. You should do what you want to – it's your day.

Seating plans

Set aside a full month to get this particular item sorted. Think compatibility, think friends who haven't seen each other for ages, but most of all, think matchmaking...

Parents

Because some couples are paying for everything themselves, they feel there is no need to refer to their elders. But it's good etiquette to involve your parents in some way, even if they aren't footing the bill.

DIY

While creativity can be a beautiful thing, there is a problem if the bride feels exhausted on the day as she has to get to the venue before everyone else to blow up the balloons. Do your own thing, by all means, but weigh up money-saving against high stress at dawn.

births

Shouting the news of your pregnancy from the rooftops is all well and good, but your close family might appreciate a face-to-face announcement. Why forgo the chance to celebrate? That bottle of champagne in the fridge will finally have its moment as your mum gets legless. Meanwhile, you will sip sparkling elderflower cordial and look radiant.

* Phone friends to tell them by all means, but again, close friends will want to share your joy with you, face to face. Think about how you would feel, and try to tell them in person. Resist the temptation to send 'I'm up the duff!' messages by text.

* When the beautiful bundle finally pops out, the husband or partner will have been given a list of 'must call' numbers. The reality is that by the time he's called the in-laws and his own parents, he'll be on his knees. Omissions are never intentional, so don't be offended if you get the news second-hand.

* Many people now make birth announcements by round robin email. While you might feel slightly short-changed, particularly if you're a very close friend, forgive them. New parents have got their hands full!

* As soon as you hear about the new arrival, send a card to congratulate the proud parents. Write something at the bottom along the lines of 'Can't wait to visit, but I'll wait to hear from you'. Everyone needs time to adjust to parenthood, so try to avoid calling during the first few days.

* Visiting mother and child in hospital is usually reserved for the immediate family, purely because time is of the essence and the new family is often home after a couple of days and ready to see visitors then.

* The first visit to the new-born is rarely done without a gift of some kind, which is why most new babies are hard to spot among mountains of teddies and soft toys. Thoughtful friends will also take a present for the mother and any small siblings who might be feeling miffed by the appearance of a rival!

* Avoid trying to guess whether someone is pregnant or not. For all you know, they are having difficulties conceiving and your champagne-swigging best mate has only turned to mineral water as part of a healthy conception drive. Even worse, someone might just be having a plump week and that baggy jumper is doing her no favours. Wait to be told!

bereavement

However confident and adept you become at dealing with all manner of situations, there will always be one that remains difficult. Death.

When you know a friend is ill, perhaps with a terminal illness, or as soon as you hear that someone close to them has died, you should act. Don't panic, worrying about what you should do or how you should help. Just write. All you need to do is tell someone that you are thinking of them. Avoid clichés. Keep it simple. Think of your friend reading the letter and remember the content is for her. After all, she's going to read the letter, not the person who has died.

It's best not to go down the 'I know how you're feeling because I know how I felt when so-and-so died' road. Instead, empathize gently without feeling the need to prove that you are well-placed to do so. And when you do see your friend, and she asks how you are, tell her – don't feel your news is irrelevant given what's she's going through. Just because you are bereaved doesn't mean that you stop thinking about what your friends are up to. Other people's news can provide a welcome distraction and help you start thinking about your own life again, particularly after a period when it feels like it's been on hold.

acknowledgments

Announcing to friends and family that I was writing a book about etiquette elicited a variety of responses. Most people were quick to remind me of various social faux pas I had committed over the years. I didn't need reminding. These things tend to stick with you.

Everyone wanted to know whether the book would really be about cutlery or how to address an admiral. When I explained that I was looking at contemporary everyday etiquette, the floodgates opened. Stories of dodgy emails, embarrassing phone calls and misjudged pregnancies as well as advice on how to manage dangerous liaisons or dump frenemies all poured out.

So I would like to thank everyone who contributed to this book: you provided me with more stories and ideas than I was eventually able to include. Thank you to my mum for 'encouraging' me – from a very young age – to start my thank-you letters the day after Boxing Day. Thank you to all of my friends for being eternally reliable, witty and kind when it comes to offering wise and generous advice when I need help and reassurance – having made a total mess of things once again.